T0157915

Chasing The Rainbow

It Could Happen To You!

FREDERICK LAWRENCE

iUniverse, Inc.
New York Bloomington

Chasing The Rainbow
It Could Happen To You!

iUniverse books may be ordered through booksellers or by contacting:

iUniverse
1663 Liberty Drive
Bloomington, IN 47403
www.iuniverse.com
1-800-Authors (1-800-288-4677)

ISBN: 978-1-4401-4722-7 (pbk)
ISBN: 978-1-4401-4723-4 (ebk)

Printed in the United States of America

iUniverse rev. date: 9/17/2009

ACKNOWLEDGMENT

Much Thanks to Trudy Pascoe for transcribing my notes and Photo's - and patience, and to Brenda Erhardt for her assistance with my computer. The book itself is a Thank You to the Musicians who were there for me.
Back Cover portrait by Robert Morrow.

All book proceeds from sales will be donated to Children with Disabilities, and other needy kids.

The CD is the culmination of my music endeavor. Recorded live March 10, 1984, "The Speakeasy", Long Beach, CA.
Bill March, Piano & Vocals - Fred Lawrence, Harmonica. Songs - Route 66 - The Summer Winds - Take the "A" Train - Satin Doll- Georgia on my Mind - I'll be seeing You - That's All.

For a Free CD please see the end of the book.

Contents

PREFACE

This is a story about music, and a wannabe musician. It also could be a story about success, as success can be measured in many ways. Success, as measured by me, is not necessarily measured by monetary gain, but in accomplishing my goal of playing jazz music, something I strived for all my life, especially in my adult years, my desire finally coming to fruition, using an instrument considered by many musicians as "not a legitimate musical instrument" – the harmonica.

It is a chronology of my musical experiences from day one, up to the present time. In the weaving of this story, there will be mention of what I call "big name" musicians, who in their time in the Big Band era were prominent musicians, and are still, in retrospect big name musicians. This is not an attempt to offer, so called name dropping, to enhance my status in playing music, but only to show the influence these people had on my life, how helpful they were with their words of encouragement, friendliness, non-criticism, inspiration, in my attempt to become a "horn player". These were simply nice people, who realized what I was attempting to do in playing jazz, and were empathetic toward me in my endeavors, in allowing me to sit in with them for a couple of "numbers". I'll always be very grateful to them. And so I mention these musicians only in the above context.

In my writing, the reader may be put off by the repetitious use of phrases, such as, "I couldn't ad lib"; improvise; I didn't know what I was doing; etc. This is simply to show the degree of ability I possessed, until the time I finally did learn to play solo improvised choruses. It is ironic, that since those early days, I have never had the opportunity to play with any "big name" musicians, I wish it were so, as I am confident I can hold my own with anyone, and realize in doing so – it is so much fun!

I have a musical photo album of my experiences, clubs, various venues, etc. Also posted in the photo album is a letter of humble thanks to all of the musicians, who encouraged, got me gigs, invited me to play with them, got me in the musicians union, a musician private club, and so much more things they did for me in my learning days. But more so than the letter of tribute, is that every time I play, my playing is also a tribute to them! God Bless all my musician friends!

CHAPTER 1
Learning by Ear

My first recollection of music is of listening to my Dad, a self-taught piano player. He also taught himself to write music in the ensuing years. He wrote many songs, none of which were successful, but he did succeed in playing piano and in learning to write music, and so lends credence to my early learning experiences. He was a good "stride" player, and during the Depression Era, worked in many piano bars for a paltry 2 dollars a nite, plus tips, which were more in the form of a glass of beer, rather than money!

In my first year of life in 1921, my earliest recollection of music was of hearing my Dad playing the piano, and like all little kids, I too would copy and imitate him, attempting to play piano. My first attempt was in crawling on the floor, and attempting to climb on the swivel piano stool, falling numerous times, until finally managing to make it. Then I would try to imitate the music he played – of course it was only with one finger! I had a "very good ear", and so would also try to play music I heard on the radio. It must have been in the very beginning that I could hear a song once, and would know the tune, and listen to the lyrics once or twice, and would know those also – even though at that age, I didn't know what the words meant!

In those days the only electricity was an overhead bulb hanging from the ceiling – there were no wall outlets. So the radio ran on an automobile battery, which had to be recharged frequently, so the only time I could hear music was when he came home from work. I became inured to all types of music, pop, opera, symphonic, and on Saturday morning – *"The Italian Hour"* on a certain radio station. One of his favorite programs was the *"Jenney Program"*, listening to the Jenney Band, sponsored by the Jenney Gasoline Corp. The featured soloist was a fine cornetist/ trumpet player named Walter Smith, and I well remember him above all others.

Also in that first year, listening to lyrics, and trying to understand what the words meant, most likely helped in my learning to talk. So I played, and listened from about age 1 to somewhere in my 4th year, and the more I listened to my Dad, the better I became at playing piano, just trying to imitate him. I got to the point of playing with two hands, imitating his chord playing, and the more I did that, the more fun it became, and my love for music grew by leaps and bounds. It has always been my #1 Love!

I also had one childhood friend whose brother was in a marching band at school, and passed down his drumming skills to his kid brother, who then taught me the various military drum beats. We would sit on the front steps of his house, wearing out the brothers drumsticks on the wooden steps, rat-tat-tatting by the hour. So I also learned about drumming before I went to kindergarten. Much later would come other lessons in drumming, big band style, and later again, lessons in bongo and conga drumming, all of which only enhanced my appreciation for various rhythms, before my 14th year.

Though my Dad tried to form a trio of three of my sisters, they only did any singing for a brief period with one radio appearance in a contest, but did not pursue music, and only as music fans from then on. And a younger brother only briefly tried the violin. He later was a D.J. at a small radio station, but was always replaced for playing his favorites, Stan Kenton, and Maynard Ferguson against the wishes of the radio station owners. He also promoted a few jazz festivals in his locale. Nobody really pursued music as I did, though I'm positive there was much latent music talent in the family.

I can still remember, as though it were yesterday, when I was in my 4th year of life, 82 years ago – I was playing the piano, by this time playing with 2 hands – my Mom and Dad standing in the doorway of our living room, and I heard my Dad say, "Jo, I think we have a genius here". It might have been the same, or the next day, when my Dad asked me if I would like to study music? "Yeah," was my quick reply. Then he asked the question that should never have been put to me! "What would you like to play"? And I immediately said, "Trombone"! The following ensued – "Trombone? Why trombone",? In a very perplexed, somewhat baffled, a bit angry and disappointed voice. And in my 4 year old mind, I simply told the truth – "cause I like the sound"---. Then in a, "I'm the boss," type of sermon, he explained. If I learned the piano, I could play any instrument. As he expounded on the virtues of the piano, I just kept repeating, "I like the trombone"– only furthering his anger and disappointment. We must have gone round and round for an hour, with the same resulting answer from this young 4 year old. What did I know? I just knew that I had watched countless parades, and was always struck by the sound of the flashing trombones in the front line of the band, and it always excited me. It still does – it is, and has always been my favorite instrument, and in later years of the 'Swing Era, I would go to hear all the big bands, and the only people I cared to meet were the trombonists in the band, and I met many, many of my favorite musicians. The upshot of my discourse by my Dad was his final statement – "Piano or nothing"! He locked up the piano from that day on, and I never saw it unlocked until I was about 14 years of age!

Looking back, I always wonder why he didn't think the reverse of his statement, if I played piano I could play anything – for in my years of listening to all types of bands and music, I have come to the realization that I love just about all instruments and would have loved to play many of them – one of my favorites being the French Horn. I know of a point in my twenties, I wish I could be a music arranger – as I love the diversity of sound – I collected all types of sounds of the big bands, until my returning home from overseas, I discovered the sound of Stan Kenton in 1945. From then on that was my band, I collected every record, album, until Stan passed away, got to know and meet just about all who ever played in his bands – culminating in meeting with Stan for many years – as though he were my second Dad! Listening to Stan Kenton, I'm sure he was the impetus of my deciding I was going to start going to clubs and try to play!

But in all fairness to my Dad, he was a good Father, devoted to his family and my Mom, and very solicitous of her, and a great helpmate. He instilled in we 8 kids, the right and wrong of living, good morals, character, and common sense, and everything necessary to be a good person. The one important thing missing was that he didn't know how to teach. Coming from, and being the first born of an Immigrant family, he was subject to much corporal punishment, of all kinds, and that is all he knew, like most immigrant families of those early days, and was mis-treated badly – and I guess it rubbed off.

He was a fine athlete, and at 15 he was a good size for his age at that time – played baseball at which he excelled, and played, what was early pro-football in the New England League, winning a championship in 1906 – at the grand pay scale of $10.00 per man! His father wanted him to work in his bakery, and when he found the football uniform under the bed, he threw a tantrum, beating my Dad, and throwing him out of the house. So at that young age, my Dad went to work on the "Banana Boats", going to and from Central America, and how I remember the bananas he brought home in my early years! So with a life-time of abuse I can understand his treatment of we kids – though unlike him, I learned from his similar treatment of me. If he wasn't taught how to raise children, his teachings would be just like his Dad. But nevertheless, there were the rare moments when I saw the inner man, and that was a likeable sincere person. I would also suppose that the Depression era days, and all that inferred was no picnic with 8 kids to worry about, and no income. A good person inside, that simply wasn't a good teacher outside. But he was my Dad, and I loved and respected him.

I'm sure the above musical episode when I was 4, was a sort of punishment, for I never studied music, even in school, it was a mystery to me – like a built in road block. To this day I can't read or write music. When playing with others I always have to ask what key we are playing in, so I can pick up the harmonica in a particular key! But I can hear it! And to that extent I often change the rhythm to a different beat, or a different style unlike the original in it's known form.

Being deprived of music early on, I devised my own instruments, making a ukulele from a cigar box with different size elastic bands, drums from old pots and pans, a bass from a box with a handle and a piece of clothesline, filled my Mom's wine glasses with varied amounts of water to make a xylophone, bought kazoos, or if no money, just use a comb covered with wax paper and hum through it, played a jews harp, anything to make music! Even started singing in clubs when I was much older, and before I began playing harmonica in the clubs.

In my early teens I had a crystal set and earphones. It was the beginning of the big band era. There was a big change in popular music. One could listen to the radio, which was akin to television today. All the main programs featured a big band, but I couldn't listen to them, as we kids were in bed before 9 PM. With my crystal set and an antenna wire hanging out of the window, I was able to pick up remote broadcasts from a good part of the country, Pittsburg, PA., Denver, Colo., Chicago, New York, etc. I would listen to Glenn Miller, Benny Goodman and so many others in their early days of being on the road, many times I'd fall asleep while listening. But it was an exciting time, and an exciting music.

Though my Dad and I had a falling out because of my choice of trombone over the piano when I was a young 4 year old, I always felt maligned by him, as nothing I accomplished, any little success I had, never made an impression on him, instead turning my positive accomplishment into a negative – he harbored an ill feeling toward me all because of this little 4 year olds choice of a musical instrument.

But little did he realize he was the instigator of my playing the harmonica. It was the middle of the Depression Era, and one day he came home, smiling and happy – he had found a job. He gave all we 8 kids 10 cents – a good sum in those days. I went to F.W. Woolworth, the famous "5 & 10 Cent Store", and bought a little Bible for a nickel, open it up, and a little snake pops out. I also bought my first harmonica for 5 cents. I was 12 years old. I started playing right away, and it was easy, the music had always been inside waiting to come out, and come out it did! I remember some of the first songs I played – There's No Place Like Home – There's a Long, Long Trail a Winding – My Old Kentucky Home – Red River Valley, many more Stephen Foster songs, western music, and what we called, "Hillbilly" music. All came naturally and very easily. Pretty soon I had all my friends playing harmonicas. I well remember playing at home, I suppose trying to impress him with my musical expertise. The upshot of that was my Dad saying, "If you're going to play that thing, go down to the cellar, or take it outside." He must have considered it an affront to him because of our earlier disagreement. He never liked to hear me play, so I learned never to play when he was home.

But I continued to play, everything came easy, and I could play *almost* everything I heard. As I became a newspaper delivery boy, I had my own income, the greater part I gave to my Mom. With my allowance and tips I began buying all kinds of harmonicas, Marine Bands, others that had a nice tremolo sound, some were double sided, and I just enjoyed making music.

Wanting to play properly, note for note, and this period being the beginning of the "Big Band" era, I naturally wanted to play big band music. Most times I found I couldn't do it, as I couldn't play the half tones in the music. The original frustrating song was "Rosalie", from a hit movie that starred Nelson Eddy and Jeanette McDonald, two of Hollywood's outstanding musical stars. The movie was a big hit and so was the song.

Working a daily paper route and also a Sunday delivery route, I was making $2.75 a week, and getting independent! I asked my Mom if I could keep one weeks pay to buy a chromatic harmonica, and she acquiesced. I went to the pawn shop where they sold all brand new Hohner harmonicas, and bought my first chromatic for $2.50!! (The same harmonica would cost 100 dollars today!) Down to the cellar I went and tried to play "Rosalie" – and what a joy to be able to play all the half-notes in that first stumbling block to play big band music! I stayed there for hours playing all the ballads of the day – even trying what I knew of opera, classical music and waltzes, whatever I knew in my keen musical mind. I was thrilled and overwhelmed by all the various musical styles I was able to play.

I also discovered an easy way to play the chromatic. The chromatic harmonica has a slide, with a button on the end. If you push the button in it gives you a half tone. Trying various tunes, I experimented with playing with the button, or slide, being in all the time, and using it in reverse to get my half tones. To me the notes had a smoother response, with a better continuity of sound, less staccato sound and an ease of playing. So I've always played with the slide in – almost like playing on the black keys of a piano and using the white keys for half tones. For me it comes very easy. Blowing and drawing in air on the notes, was also much easier. To my great joy, many years later, I discovered my playing in this way gave me all the flat keys jazz musicians use – so when I played in clubs many years later, I was ready and equipped to play in any jazz key they wanted! But that comes much later in my many years of attempting to play jazz, improvised, ad-lib solos, which I will relate as you read on.

My Dad didn't realize that he did have an effect on my playing. For countless days I heard him practicing a piano piece called "Nola". It is a tricky piece, and demands a great deal of talent. I understood in his repetitious playing of this piece, he was a perfectionist, he put demands on himself musically, that was praiseworthy. Hearing him and his dedication to perfection rubbed off on me, and that was my reason for buying my chromatic – I wanted every note perfect. Later on in playing jazz music, I would learn to play songs a different way, but never the less, even though improvised choruses are not the note-for-note music as written, one has to play within the context of the song, and play a solo that makes musical sense.

The most difficult songs to play, are songs with key changes, and I stay away from them – unless I am improvising, which allows me to 'play around' the changes, which works out fine and doesn't destroy the content of the song or solo. For key changes, in playing not for note, it changes your breathing pattern in and out, and also changes the pushing in and out of the slide – everything normal changes, so being a note for note perfectionist, I'd rather play another tune, rather than play a tune very badly. All harmonicas are made to play one key only, hence the various keys from A to G that are made by the manufacturer. I think I was 50 years old before I found that harmonicas were made in all keys, and not only in C and G that I had been buying for years.

In the early years of playing, I was frequently reminded of my Dad, when I'd come up against one of these songs with key changes that I couldn't master. I would consider myself a failure because I hadn't studied music, and would often think of my Dad and my lost opportunity to learn music, which was so dear, and in my blood and my soul.

Long before I ever decided to take my harmonica into the

clubs, I along with friends, used to do a lot of singing in the bars that had a piano player (as my Dad) and an open mike. Anyone could sing at any time. I did that for 10 years or so. I must revert back at this point to reveal a major part of my lack of trying to play, or sing.

In my early teens, when my Dad was playing piano in bars for a few extra dollars, he very frequently asked me to teach him songs he didn't know, that were very popular in the 30's, and most were big band songs.

For a couple of years he tried to get me to sing. But because of his attitude toward me, regarding our confrontation when I was 4 years old, there remained a rift in our relationship which only steadily grew. We had no rapport – any of my perceived success at anything I did was always met with a curt remark. The constant treatment of this sort built a very strong feeling of ineptness in me, affecting my school work and the negative feeling of self worth. Inhibited, shy, very self conscious – I had a big problem. So when he would ask me to sing – I didn't want to. This would result in a slap, furthering my resentment, and disinclination to sing. Who would feel like singing in that situation? I loved and respected my Dad, but didn't feel that he reciprocated in any way – he wasn't my friend – so I reacted as I did, by refusing to sing – it wasn't enjoyable.

So after this period of a year or two, and when he asked me to teach him a song, I never sang it – I always whistled it. Later on I frequented a place where a good friend of my Dad's also played piano. I was so inhibited from the above experiences – I sat and listened for 2 years before I had guts enough to get up and sing!

To indicate the relationship between my Dad and I – I was singing in another club with my Dad's friend Dick. During a break, unknown to me, Dick had gone to another bar a block away from where we were, and where my Dad was tending bar in a Tavern, which closed early. He had brought my Dad in to hear me sing. After I did, Dick made me aware of my Dad's opinion of my singing. It was another of his denigrating remarks – "No poise"! I wasn't surprised, but the degree of hurt wasn't as bad as previously felt by me, for by this time I was beginning to overcome my inhibitions, and though no Bob Eberle, Dick Haymes, or Sinatra, people liked my singing, which gave me the impetus to continue.

Surprise Family at 1983 at Air Force Reunion, playing with Ted Herbert Big Band- Danvers MA.

CHAPTER 2
Adventures in Music

Over the ensuing years, I played by myself, most times at home, practicing new songs, or difficult rhythms, especially Latin or Bossa Nova which I love. Much of this was done when alone, the only exception being when I would play for my infant children, as I held them in my arms, my reveling in their bugeyed transfixed stares, as I played them to sleep. Many years went by before I decided to hit the clubs.

There were only 2 occasions when I played a lot. The first being in the C.C.C. (Civilian Conservation Corps), a Government program to give jobs to men during the Depression, working in forests, National Parks, etc. I played music for the guys in the barracks at night before lights out, occasionally someone would join in with a guitar.

Also in WWII in my barracks at night, and later overseas when we put on a show we wrote, and where I was a featured soloist with our 10 piece band, doing 9 shows in 7 days in Naples, Italy, for the Red Cross, Hospitals, playing at an Opera House and the Palm Theatre, the Royal Air Force among others. Probably the most important event at that time was in playing for the 310th Bomb Group of the 12th Air Force, in which after playing my initial tune – I got 3 encores!! I was really into playing by this time. Some years after the war, in telephoning a buddy in New Jersey, he told me, "Fred, every time we moved to a new air base, I always pitched my tent next to yours so I could hear you play". That was a real heartwarming tribute from a good buddy.

During this same time, not being able to fly missions because of bad weather, we wrote letters, read books, etc., to kill time, as the weather was so bad, most times we only left the tent to go to "chow", or answer the call of nature. Having nothing to occupy myself, I compiled a list of all the songs I knew, most of which I could play. So at age 24 I knew 1100 songs, and probably forgot to list others I couldn't recollect at that time.

Two things stand out in my mind of my Air Force WWII days. One was an occasion in Italy, which I will relate secondly, for it is much more important, and a lesson learned about freedom.

In coming home from Italy after the conclusion of the War, some of us Air Force guys were asked to volunteer for K.P. (kitchen police) in the galley of our troop ship. Ground forces from a tank destroyer outfit were doing all the KP, while our higher ranking Air Force personnel lounged around. I was one to volunteer, and in entering the galley, some one was playing a harmonica. I asked if I could borrow it, my request being granted. I played a couple of tunes for the guys, and the head honcho of the galley came up to me and said, "See that pile of bags of sugar over there? Well, you climb up on that pile of sugar, and play! – don't do any thing except play!" So for a week I pulled KP – Just playing music until we reached our destination at home, Boston, Mass., where I had enlisted nearly 4 years before – and the first time I had seen it from the day I enlisted December 19, 1941!

A most important event regarding music occurred in our early days in Italy. A Buddy of mine from Pennsylvania and I took a ride down a road just to see where it went. We entered a town where people had never seen American soldiers before. To be brief we went to this town for weeks, being the only Americans there, and in this time made excellent friends with the people, who were destitute. We had a great time, supplied them with food, candy, cigarettes like all "G.I.'s" do in war. They were a great people, giving of the little they had, wonderful to know.

The following is taken from my book of WWII experiences – *"Untold & Unsung – the Unknown"*.

One day my old friend Gene Kmetovicz came to the tent, suggesting we take a ride on his German motorcycle. Acquiescing, we packed whatever goodies we had in a musette bag, Gene deciding to follow a road 'to see where it went'. After riding some miles we came to the outskirts of a town called Francovilla. We stopped, and immediately all the people on the street, ran into their houses, bolting the doors and shutters. All except one young boy. We were on a German motorcycle, and our suntan uniforms resembled the German's in color. *"Tedeschi"*? (German) hollered the boy to us. "No", we answered. *"Inglese"?,* came another loud question. "No…American"!, we hollered back. Jumping up and down, the boy kept yelling, "American! American"!…and all the people came out of their houses to greet us with hugs and kisses, handshakes, blessing themselves and thanking God and the Americans, We were the first Americans they had seen. I've never seen a happier people in my life…they couldn't get enough of us, and we quickly started giving away much of what we had in the musette bag.

The young boy dashed off to the center of town, and we followed slowly, the ever growing crowd marveling at the 'new *Americani soldati*', pressing close to touch us, or to shake hands, showering us with flowers, *"Viva Americani"!* being shouted over and over again. We were escorted to an Italian restaurant, where we were fed chicken, *vino* and bread, the only food available, as we were soon to learn, the people were destitute, but they gave us all they had, eagerly watching as we very humbly ate their offering. This very new experience awakened something in me I hadn't experienced since I lost my plane and crew. These people were broke, no food, jobs or future, many of their husbands, sons, brothers, fathers, dead or in captivity somewhere, many missing… and they were filled with hope and faith…we were like Angels from Heaven to them. I had nearly lost all those qualities they displayed.

Soon a large group of Italian soldiers appeared, marching down the street, stopping in front of the restaurant. We went outside to observe the first Italian soldiers we had seen. The Captain of the group, saluted us explaining, "I'm the commander of the local garrison, and I would like to surrender my sword to you". Evidently, being a small garrison of 250 or so Italian troops, who were essentially out of the war, the 5th Army had just by-passed them, pursuing the Germans instead.

Gene and I discussed this amazing flattering offer, and decided it would be rather embarrassing for this officer to surrender to a couple of rear echelon sergeants, so Kmetovicz, outranking me, gave what we thought a very appropriate face-saving reply to the Captain. "Thank you, Sir", saluting smartly, "I think it appropriate you give your sword to another American officer who will be knowledgeable as to proper procedures in such matters". "Thank you, my American Sergeant, then may I welcome you to our lovely Francovilla, and our Italian people. You are always welcome here, whatever you wish is yours". All this spoken by both sides, a little Italian we knew, and the sparse English spoken by, and interpreted by those in the crowd who understood and were able to translate all. At this the soldiers threw their hats in the air cheering us, shouting, *"Viva Americano…Viva America"*!! Then we had a parade, all around the streets and town, with Gene and I leading, followed by the Italian Captain and his garrison, and by this time the whole town knew of us, and lined the sidewalks, cheering, clapping till we got back to the restaurant where much *vino* was consumed by all, much singing and dancing ensued, I met a pretty Italian girl named "Michelina," and we had one big party.

For many weeks Gene and I had the town all to ourselves,

sneaking off unobserved, to partake of all that was offered us, and then some! And always we would see our mess Sergeant Manny Robello, and take whatever he could spare of food, and bring it to the people of Francovilla, plus the rations we had of cigarettes, soap, chocolate...everything the people hadn't had in years.

Rather than being in the center of town, we always visited the Italian people we had met the first day, one couple owning a wine cellar, with great big wine vats, and where many people had lunch, wine and a chunk of bread! We enjoyed our visits with our new friends until one day, someone followed us, wondering where we disappeared to. That blew it for us, and immediately the town saw a great many GIs from the base, and too many GIs are like too many cooks in the kitchen.

One day the owner of the wine cellar told us we were moving, which we denied. He insisted, even though we hadn't had any word of a move. He said we were moving to Foggia. Try as we might we couldn't convince him we weren't moving. But he was adamant, and as we had so unselfishly given the Italian people much in our visits to Francovilla, they wanted to give us a going away party, and for us to return the following Friday. A few days later, we got word to prepare to move. Where? Foggia!

Gene and I invited about 15 men to our party...including Capt. Lord, who I figured might like me a bit more, without brown=nosing...as he was the twin of my buddy, schoolmate and next door neighbor. I can show friendship, but I wouldn't kiss anyone's foot for anything...hence I invited Capt. Lord, along with all the other mechanics, as he was our boss.

We had a great dinner, chicken, rabbit, brown spaghetti, made from rye, as there was no white flour in all of Italy, no cheese, sauce made from the cans of stewed tomatoes we had given to them...everything they owned they gave to us! And everything was delicious. Much *vino* was consumed, and I found myself standing on a big round table, playing on my harmonica, all the Italian songs I knew, Santa Lucia, O'Sole Mio, even Amapola!

While playing I heard a sobbing tenor, and looking down saw

a man who looked like Jimmy Durante, singing his heart out, tears streaming down his face, the Mayor, Chief of Police, and other civil dignitaries were all emotional in their singing. When I stepped off the table, I asked my Italian host why everyone was crying and sad...we were supposed to be having a good time. His reply to me was, "This is the first time we have been allowed to sing in 10 years"! He then recounted to me the murders, torture, beatings and arrests Italians suffered from the Germans if they saw a group of people together, surmising some type of Italian conspiracy, or spies...even two people talking together were subject to any type of treatment the Germans saw fit to impose...from imprisonment to murder!

What I had taken for granted all my life in America, now became my first lesson in what freedom really meant! For all time I keep asking in wonderment, "They couldn't even sing"?

Perhaps I should state here that my main occupation was as a heavy duty mechanic, having started in the Air Force in WWII – music was my main hobby. As a mechanic, I had only one work ethic, do your job right, do it as fast as you can, do it once! So I applied the same thing to playing music.

After the war there was never the encouragement or incentive, or any opportunity to play music, again only occasionally when alone at home.

Although listening to, and playing all types of music in the beginning years, blues, western, so-called hillbilly music, and having an interest in all types of music, I as most of my compatriots, became addicted to Big Band music. And they played everything, as the above. My appreciation of classical and opera concerto's came about by listening to the Big Bands playing many of these songs in their various renditions of this beautiful music. Increasingly so, I wanted to play big band music, and after the war I heard a new band the first day I returned from overseas – Stan Kenton's 'Artistry Jumps'! I fell in love with the Kenton sound, and forever more I wanted to play like the Kenton Band!

Being addicted to the big bands, one could hear the music on any number of radio stations, juke boxes in restaurants, stores, wherever one went, there was the music, plus all the records I had collected since my teen years. I was drowning in the sound, and had been for years. Even in the Depression's sad years, the music was there, probably the most important aspect of life, in itself uplifting, the beautifully simple ballads, the jump tunes, or just the pop tunes. There's a saying that encourages "The music that got us through the War." I personally think the music gets us through life! Imagine a world without music! No matter it being sad, happy, or whatever it's type, a world without music would be a lost world!

In my teen years there were many times we went to see and hear the big bands who were only sounds on radio or recordings, so to see them in person was a great experience. I would always be down front, close to the bandstand watching and listening to my idols play. My buddies learned to do all sorts of "jitterbugging" and other dance steps – I never did – I just wanted to watch and listen to all the music they played. I made a point to meet many of them – especially the trombonists! I met many of the leaders, and became friends with many musicians who's records I would collect. In a club I always invited them for a drink at my table – especially trombonists. To this day I still love the trombone, and if there is one sound I like equally well, it is the French Horn.

CHAPTER 3
Jazz—The Learning Years

I had three desires in playing music. I wanted to play pretty, like Bobby Hackett, featured in the Glenn Miller Band, and other aggregations, small groups, and bands of his own. Featured on Jackie Gleason recordings – a fine horn man, and one of my favorites.

I wanted to "swing" like Benny Goodman, one of the most successful of all the big bands, who's records I collected for years.

I wanted to sound like Stan Kenton's band, my favorite band and leader. Stan influenced my musical thinking, and I was privileged to meet him many times, and knew many of the men in the band, one trombonist, Dick Shearer, and I became good friends for years.

There are many music stories and events that occurred in the ensuing years I would like to relate, but will save those for another time. I will attempt to hold these happenings to my long road in trying to play jazz, and soloing improvisational choruses. I would also like to reiterate, any "names" of well known musicians mentioned here, are not at all for the enhancement of me or my playing, or "name dropping". These are the people I met mostly by chance, and how they helped me with encouraging words – always. For if any one of them had put me down – I'm sure I would have quit playing. So my eternal thanks to all of these great musicians, "names" or not, for their encouragement.

One of the earliest influences in my early attempts at playing music was Sabby Lewis. Sabby had a nine piece band in Boston, and was highly regarded as a pianist, arranger and band leader.

There was a popular radio show called *the "Fitch Band Wagon"*. Fitch was, and probably still is, a top manufacturer of hair shampoo. The show featured a different big band every week. Some well known, and others unknown. Sabby's band appeared for the one week show – and stayed for 6 months! That had never happened before, and it catapulted Sabby into musical fame. Sabby was lionized in Boston and New York, playing at all the famous jazz clubs, even gaining top billing over Ella Fitzgerald, the Ink Spots, and other highly rated musical greats – I saw these club fliers and ads in Sabby's Scrapbook.

Sabby appeared many years later with a trio in a club in my town. I went to hear him and was immediately taken with his fine playing. I saw him often,, got to know him, and became great friends. I won't go into details of all our years of friendship, only to say I met many other fine musician friends of Sabby's, shared many years together, in many venues, and marveled at his command of the piano. I never tired of listening to him play. Many years later I found an LP of his band, a rarity, and donated it to his Archive, set up upon his death, at Boston University. Sabby was a musical icon in New England. I will never forget him or the great influence he had on my playing music. Ironically, we never played together, as he was one that didn't think of a harmonica being a jazz instrument. And in those days I didn't know how to play jazz, so never asked him if I could sit in. Still, it was knowing and listening to Sabby, and the final resolve I had to go to the clubs and try to play the music I loved – jazz! Thanks Sabby, for everything!

The very first time I went to a club to play music was at the "Bali Lounge", at Revere Beach, Mass., an area similar to New York's Coney Island. The trio let me sit in, so I did "Stella by Starlight", and got a nice response. So I did "Over the Rainbow", and again received a nice receptive round of applause. I went back there a few times, then the owner of another club invited me to his club, "The Sands". I played there only a few times, and it was a short stint of playing in the clubs, but a nice start. It was a few years before I played a club again.

Jumping ahead some years after the above, I had moved to another area, and on one of my infrequent stops for a cold beer after work, I was in a beer joint, relaxing, when a man played a number on the juke box. It was a fine trumpet solo, long forgotten now – but I asked him who the trumpet player was. He told me, and then said, "If you want to hear a good trumpet player, listen to Maynard Ferguson". I said, "Oh, I've got a great collection of Maynard's, in fact I met him a few times, even sharing drinks at a dance, and a few other sessions." From then on my new friend, Ed Main, who just happened to be a fine trumpet player, and I became good friends.

He invited me to an old, beautiful 1700's dinner house in Monponset, Mass., where he had a six piece group. In following visits we talked a great deal about music. As I was quite knowledgeable about music, he asked me what instrument I played, assuming I was a musician. I said, "I don't play a horn, I just play a harmonica, but love playing big band tunes". Ed said, "Bring it in". So I did, and that was my main introduction in my attempt to play jazz. I was OK with ballads, but trying to do a solo on jump tunes—I was completely lost! Ed let me play full sets every time I went to the Inn, and in telling Ed I couldn't play jazz solo's, he would say, "Fake it" – so I did, failing most of the time. But it was a good learning experience. Unlike Ed Main, I had been to countless clubs in my adult years, and never saw a musician come into a club, and get an invitation to "sit in". So I felt indeed fortunate Ed always had me join in with playing with the band.

Ed had a neck injury, due to an auto accident, so the tenor sax man took over the band, Jack De Chambreau. I liked Jack's playing, as he reminded me of Duke's man, Paul Gonsalves, whom I met at an all night party with my buddy Sabby Lewis. The following anecdote is one of many reasons I kept trying to play.

One night when playing with the group, a fellow came up asking us to play "Ruby", which was a #1 hit in music. The harmonica player on that hit record was Richard Hayman. It so happens, whenever the band mentioned my name in playing, they would refer to me as "Dick Hymen", a musicians inside joke, referring to a woman's private parts,—so this customer kept asking for "Ruby" all night. I didn't want to play it as I had forgotten the "bridge" to the song – so refused at every set we played. Finally on the fourth and final set, he asked again, and my refusal got a 'fake it', from Jack – so I did, but changed the tune to a Latin beat! Everything worked out well for a change. While sitting at the table having a final drink, this customer came over to us, apologizing for pestering us for 'Ruby'. He said, "We're celebrating our wedding anniversary, and that was 'our song' we heard often on our honeymoon – He said to me – assuming I was Richard Hayman – "You know you played Ruby better than you did on the record"!! What a compliment! Wow! I thanked him for the compliment – but knowing in my mind I didn't even know what I had played, just whatever came to my head. Most importantly was the fact of the words to me, and one of the first times encouraging words helped me to decide to keep trying to play jazz.

Another incident regarding Ed Main which was very important in my early attempt to play jazz. This took place on a visit back to Massachusetts to visit my family, after relocating to California a few years later. (More on that further on.) I decided to visit Ed in his new home in Plymouth, Mass., we had a nice time reminiscing. One thing I knew about Ed was that he 'told it like it is' – he never held back, but spoke from his heart, an honest person all the way. I remembered an incident of a customer requesting we play a song Bert Kampfurt made famous. Ed didn't like Bert, the European Trumpeter, and he told the customer, in an angry tone, ' Bert Kampfurt '----'"!! He slammed down his horn, and he and the band walked off the stage! He sure did tell it like it is!!

So these few years later I asked him, "How come you let me sit in when I didn't know what I was doing?" Ed replied, "Because you were good, and the people liked it"! So coming from a guy like Ed, who was the most outspoken, and severe music critic I have ever met, that said I had something to offer, so again an encouragement to keep trying to play jazz. I owe much to Ed, my early champion!

One of many Jazz groups I have played with at
Air Force Reunions. San Diego CA. 1976

CHAPTER 4
California Sounds of Jazz

Due to an unsatisfactory life in Massachusetts I decided to go to California. I got employment very quickly – I was 48 years old. Making more money, and with less overhead, I began to cruise the clubs looking for a place to play. It seemed there was a club on every corner in my area of Huntington Park.

The very first club I played in, "The Tami Ami", had a piano guitar duo, and they let me join them. They liked my playing and I did so for a few weeks, also playing with them at the Hollywood Hyatt Hotel, in which an incident occurred to further my attempts at playing.

The table next to the piano bar was occupied by an elderly man, and a very young beautiful girl. I had played a few songs, and the man and woman left the room. A few minutes later he returned and came up to me saying, "I had to come back to tell you how much I enjoyed your playing, thank you". Wow! Imagine this guy coming back to thank me!! I was amazed and overwhelmed! To me another sign of, "I must be doing something right"! These two friends told me of other clubs to visit where I could sit in.

So, one of my long term associations was with the "Majestic" in Huntington Park. I met a fine person and pianist, Arnie Berquist, formerly from Sweden, I think. He came to America some years before with Rolf Ericson, a fine trumpet and featured soloist whom I met in '58 when he was playing with Stan Kenton. He was also featured with Woody Herman.

It was with Arnie I really got started, playing every weekend, sometimes playing bongos, or a snare drum with him, doing a bit of singing also. Arnie, good friend, would also tell me of other places to go where I could sit in. So began my quest in earnest, to find musicians and clubs to play, hoping someday I could learn to improvise jazz choruses.

One club Arnie told me about was the "Dixiebelle", in Downey, the first club that featured jazz musicians. Buddy Banks was the piano player, and Al Morgan was the bass player. On meeting Al, I learned he had been in the Sabby Lewis band, so I met an unexpected friend, said friendship lasted until Al passed away on an Easter morning in the 70's. Al knew I couldn't play jazz, but he was the most encouraging, always standing in back of me while I was playing – and saying up close in my ear – "yeah, that's it, you got it, yeah keep going, that's the way", so many words of encouragement, that even though I didn't know what I was doing, I was picking things up, bit by bit – only because of guys like Al encouraging, and a friend also. I often wonder if I would get the same nice treatment if I had been a struggling sax player? I played with Buddy for years, even after Al passed away. From Buddy I learned a bit about piano men. All had their favorite keys, a few were limited, some only playing in one or two keys, so in a way, they were as limited as I! Another thing I learned, black musicians had a different approach, so I had to apply my own feelings into the music. Playing other instruments, one can 'slide' to other notes, one can't do that on a chromatic harmonica, so I had to try to get that effect as best I could. But Buddy and

Al were both responsible for boosting me on the road to learning to play jazz.

I would like to interject at this point, a couple of things relating to the above people, and their musical successes and also how they helped me.

Sabby Lewis, though successful early on with his 'big band' did not remain in that niche. But those in his band did go on to bigger things in the music field. "Cat" Anderson, who went on to play with Duke Ellington for 28 years. Duke's featured sax player, Paul Gonsalves, who played 58 choruses straight, without repetition at the Newport Jazz Festival, Sam Woodyard, also one of Duke's drummers, Harry Carney, Duke's baritone horn man, and others I'm not sure of, as many of Duke's band were Boston and other towns in Mass. people. Sonny Stitt, Illinois Jacquette were also from Sabby's band, as Al morgan mentioned above. Sabby led some other groups in Boston, Big and Small, was a favorite DJ and was very prominent in the arts, holding many jazz festivals – a real icon!

I must mention Buddy Banks, who helped me a great deal – he got me my Musicians Union card in Los Angeles, got me a membership in the 'Clef Club', an association of retired and still active musicians, some who were early players in New Orleans and Memphis who had moved to Los Angeles, also getting me a spot on the program at my first jazz festival in Monterey Park, CA., even though I still wasn't a good jazz player. Buddy was typical of the many musicians who helped me in my quest to play music.

My making a good wage enabled me to visit many clubs on the weekends where Buddy, Al, Arnie played, and I may be able to sit in for a couple of numbers. I never played more than 2 or 3 numbers – I didn't want to wear out my welcome, and this habit usually resulted in being invited to return again.

One negative trip I took to a black nightclub, by a female black drummer who occasionally played with Arnie, suggested I go to the "Parisian Room" in downtown Los Angeles. I went there, sat at the separated bar, independent of the lounge area. I

Frederick Lawrence

listened to the great music, and asked the bartender if I could take my drink into the lounge. Getting his OK I went in and heard one of the best tenor sax players I had ever heard. Thinking I can't play with him, he was unknown to me, but I wasn't about to make a fool of myself by trying to play jazz with his group – I couldn't touch them musically! Red Holloway the tenor man eventually became famous as he is great. I left the club later, very cognizant of my musical shortcomings. That is the only time I realized I'd better not try to play with these heavyweights – I just didn't know how!

Another time I went to play in a club called "The 940 Club", probably the address of the lounge, located next door to Alan Hale Jr's, "Lobster Barrel". I had seen an ad in the *LA Times* that Dick Carey was playing there. I remembered seeing Dick Carey and Bobby Hackett in 1945 in a club in Everett, Mass., on a few occasions, so thought maybe he'd let me play. By this time I had met Bobby Hackett through my brother when I went to see him on Cape Cod, and I listened to Bobby's great horn and Dave McKenna's wonderful jazz piano.

I went to the club, told Dick Carey how I remembered him, and of meeting Bobby Hackett – after talking awhile I asked to play – they kept looking for my instrument, and when I pulled out my harmonica, I could tell by the look on their faces they didn't want me to play. But I think Dick thought, if he refused me, I'd relay that fact to Bobby, so he let me do a couple of numbers, only "Over the Rainbow" sounding good. The other was a jump tune, and I got lost in the solo, but managed to make a good finish! After that semi-fiasco I talked to all the guys in the group – none of these famous jazz musicians said one word of a negative comment. I helped the sax player with his multinous horns, and the drummer out with his gear, loading it into their cars. All I heard was, "stay with it, you'll be OK", "you did OK, keep at it", and other encouraging remarks – nothing of a negative nature, what great guys! Now I knew one thing that made them the great players they were – they were also great guys!

I drove home 100 feet above the freeway – that's how "high" I felt. Though I've never used drugs playing – music gets me high. And do you know why I was so high? I had played with my idols – guys I had listened to all my life, playing in the big bands I loved! The two lesser known men were Dick Carey playing an 'F' trumpet, Ray Sherman, piano, Eddie Safranski, Stan Kenton's bass player, Nick Fatool, Benny Goodman's long time drummer, Herbie Harper, trombonist with many big bands, Matty Matlock, sax and other woodwinds, Bob Crosby Band alumnus, who also wrote early big band hits, and Mannie Klein, who not only played with big bands, but was a featured trumpet player in Studio Bands and in well known Hollywood musicals!! Who wouldn't be high? Who wouldn't be thrilled – even another well known musician would be happy to play with such a group! That is a highlight for me in my long road to play jazz! I'll never forget the thrill!

There are times when someone who is, or was famous, I would meet and offer a nice comment. I only mention this as a point as how a compliment from some one would help me resolve to keep playing.

Early on in Huntington Park, I played for a while at the Santa Maria restaurant, with an organ player, who left shortly after we met, when he signed a recording contract with a well known company. After playing "Love Letters", and returning to the bar, a fellow told me how much he had enjoyed my playing. We talked awhile and I learned he was Bobby Breen a child prodigy vocalist who had been featured on the *Eddie Cantor Radio Show* with Deana Durbin, she also starred in movies, as a young teenage singer. I mention this to show that to get compliments from musical people is probably more important than compliments from other people – my thinking being musical people are more prone to recognize musical ability than other less talented. Nonetheless, any comment of good performance is always welcomed.

George Reed was one of my early musician friends and excellent drummer, as well as a fine vocalist. George was a great aid in my learning to play. There were so many times in trying to improvise, I would get lost in the solo, as I didn't know what I was doing. But George had a way of playing drums that were a "musical" sound, and I would listen to his drums and immediately know where I was in the song, and pick it up and make good exit for whatever we were playing. He would always call me when he had a new gig, so I could sit in with him.

Another early booster was George Mason, electric bass player. George was electric himself as he was a boisterous, happy guy especially so for me when I was playing, always leading the applause and calling for encores. George also made sure I attended a once a year party in Harbor City, and led the cheering section, making sure I got to solo, and pick songs I wanted to play. He always got me to the forefront in playing with musicians I didn't know: a good friend and very exuberant cheerleader for me.

The people who ran the party were from Mexico, owners of a ranch. They came to LA every year just to have a jam session in their second home, they loved jazz. When the party broke up the host said, "we would meet again next year, and don't forget to bring the harmonica player"! Well that was an unexpected compliment! And I did go back the following year.

I realized in listening to tapes I made of the party music, how bad I thought I was. Listening critically, I heard my too loud amplified harmonica, not so good solo's, some fair musical thoughts in backing some other musicians or vocals, hoping listening to my wannabe self, I could learn from my mistakes.

But listening to the tapes and how bad I thought I sounded, I was aware that nobody criticized me in any way. There was one trombone player who doubled on flute, was especially aware of my inexperience but was very encouraging of my attempts at my very first jam session, and was complimentary in every thing I played. He was typical of musicians who always encouraged me in my early attempts at playing jazz. I am so indebted to these people who were so helpful: I have to assume that my being so knowledgeable about music, and at least sounding good on ballads, that I was also one who had studied music. But I didn't know doodly squat about music. All I knew was what was in my heart, soul, and head. I didn't know how to read or write music. My music school was my "ear"! I had a natural gift for music that my Dad knew early in my life, and also I.

I must not forget one of my first boosters, Don Peterson. Don was talented, being a multi-instrumentalist, drumming, piano, woodwinds and brass horns, and played them all well.

I went to a music store about 1971 to buy a new harmonica. In discussing harmonica players, I remarked on how great I thought these harmonica players were, being able to play songs in different keys on one harmonica. Don was the man behind the counter. He said, "They don't play all these songs on one harmonica, they use harmonica's in all the keys made". I replied, "I didn't know they made them in different keys, I've only seen C's and G's". So he showed me the catalogue, and there they were from A to G! What an eye opener! I told Don I play with the button in, so he helped me pick out what I needed, and in the process I bought all the harmonica's that gave me the jazz keys "A flat" on up to "F". What a lucky thing for me in learning to play the harmonica backward!

So what had been my playing in "C" sharp, or a "D" minor, with the only harmonica I owned, now became whatever key the piano player wanted, and this I am sure is the reason I was liked by other musicians. Instead of playing every song in my one lone key – now I could play in five keys THEY liked. It took me many years before I learned that important item, and have no doubt that's the reason for my popularity with them, despite my not being a good jazz player. But it became more fun, and though I don't understand the written music, I would ask what key we would be playing in, the piano player or other musicians would hold up 2 or 3 fingers, and I learned 2 was B flat, 3 fingers, E flat, and so on. Thank God they never gave me THAT one finger!

I got to know Don Peterson very well, he introduced me to clubs he played in, and so went to the "Hillside" in Long Beach, and also the "Driftroom", and that was my main start in learning to play jazz, as in these clubs, instead of a duo, I usually played with a group.

The Driftroom had a 6-7 piece group including 2 tenor sax players. One night I went in, and Norm the drummer leader told me his 2 tenor men were sick, and he wanted ME to take their place! *ME? Replace two excellent tenor-saxes?* Remember – I always felt inhibited and intimidated, but the experiences with my Dad, always feeling inadequate, so to take the place of these two men was a real feeling of not being up to doing this, but Norm said, "Just play straight ahead, play what you know". And so I did, and it was a great night for me, my first big attempt at playing lead with a group – and everything worked out well audience wise, and also musically, even switching to playing bongos on a couple of Latin tunes! Norm was satisfied with my performance, and I even more so. I played the next week-end also, as the tenor men were still sick. It is one experience I'll never forget! I even played "rock" music, something I'd never played before, as I don't particularly care for that type of music, but it was popular at the time, and jazz musicians can play anything anyway! I had Don Peterson to thank, he was an early good friend. During the week I would visit his own little music shop he ran, "Swing-Inc.", where he led three rehearsal bands, all 16 piece outfits, and so that increased my knowledge of other musicians and other clubs where I could play. Very formative years in music for me.

Both Georges, Reed and Mason called me one night, wanting me to come play music with them. At the time my Mom and 2 sisters were visiting me. It was a bad night, raining buckets, and would be a long cross town drive to Santa Monica. As my Mom and siblings were willing to go along in the inclement weather, we headed for the Motel, which featured a nice sized jazz room on Ocean Avenue. Upon my arrival I learned that "Cat" Anderson, long time Duke Ellington trumpet player was the featured musician!

Listening to "Cat" and his magnificent horn, I was surprised by my 2 George's when they asked me to play with "Cat" Anderson.

I said, "You're kidding! I can't play with him – I'm not good enough to be on the same stage with him". But they kept insisting I could do it. After much entreaties, and my reluctance, I got up to play.

Everything was going OK in my playing, with Cat and I swapping choruses, until doing an old tune called "Old Folks", a slow quite kind of bluesy song, George left the stage and started wandering about the audience, leaving me playing alone on the stage! I must admit playing alone scared me a bit, and I did my best, and the tone was fine, with Cat joining in for the take-out of the song. Cat applauded saying it was the best harmonica he had ever heard ---! Imagine that! I was dubious, and hoped that his compliment was sincere, and not just a compliment to make me feel good! That was the first time my Mom and sisters heard me play, and they were pleasantly surprised and effusive in their praise and also meeting all of the musicians.

Afterward I met Hugh Bell a fine sax man, who I had played with at the aforementioned private party, and Cat Anderson. I told him of my long friendship with Sabby Lewis, and his inspiring me to finally try my hand at playing jazz. With the many reminiscences of Sabby and Boston, we had an enjoyable night, and certainly for me, one of the best musical experiences of my life!

I would have to say that the finest friend I met in all of my club playing was Bill March, an excellent pianist, with a nice following of fans and other musicians, great sense of humor, and a wonderful human being. Bill was a good friend of Marty Paich, one of the icons of the music world, as Marty was a great arranger, had his own bands and worked with many of the great jazz vocalists, and top notch musicians in the country. Bill had worked with Marty on the Stan Kenton Neophonic orchestra project. Bill March was a few notches above any piano player I'd played with. I met him at one of the many "Fireside" cocktail lounges I had played in with other musicians. He was a bit daunting when I first played with him, and it was only after sitting in with him in the "Fireside" lounge in Downey, CA., did I get to know his style, and a beginning of a long very happy musical relationship with him.

Bill was playing with a small group led by drummer Moses Washington, with other guys who would come to the club to sit in. I would also stop in on weekend nights, as I made my rounds of various clubs "to do my thing". Barbara Sherman also would be there, and I began to do back-up playing for her, as she was a long time jazz vocalist, and she liked my back-up playing. So much so, that after knowing and playing for and with her, she gave me a Stan Kenton/Four Freshmen album for a Christmas present! She knew I was a Kenton fan.

Sometime later I met Bill, who was working at the Konakai dinner house in La Brea, CA. I began to visit Bill more often, and stay the whole nite, rather than going from club to club. Playing with Bill was easier, I played more and more as the friendship grew, and slowly began to pick up bits and pieces of music listening to him play, along with the many musicians who came in to "sit in".

It got to a point where instead of me picking up on what Bill was doing and incorporating these little musical nuances into my playing, Bill was picking up on what I was playing, and using it in his playing! All of this happening nightly was a pleasant, flattering surprise, and a great feeling for me – to think that a musician of Bill's caliber was imitating me! What a wonderful confidence builder that was.

The sharing of musical ideas in playing was a niche higher for me. Maybe Bill felt he could nurse me along so I could play a jazz solo with some continuity – something that made musical sense, as despite my musical growth, I still couldn't play a good jazz solo.

As stated previously, at age 24 I had a repertoire of over 1100 songs. Whenever I played, or wherever the club, I always attempted to play some thing different from the previous visit to any club. By the time of my playing music from the 50's to the 80's, my musical "book" had more than quadrupled, so that now, instead of playing only big band tunes, I was playing a few jump tunes, Latin songs, loved bossa nova – and of course all the pretty ballads that had been sung and played up to that time – I'm always learning musically. There weren't too many times I repeated songs, only if someone requested, or something that I felt I played well, especially playing in a club for the first time.

I remember going to a dinner house in Downey, CA – "Marmacs" – I must have played there for 4-5 years with Buddy Banks, Rex Davis and various other musicians. At this time Mal Langan, keyboard and Len Rivera bass, we the musical duo. They invited me to play, with the announcement of – "Here's Fred – he's been coming here 2 years and he never plays the same song twice"! Which was very true.

One important thing I began to realize, was the audience. I always played for the people, not only for me. The songs I chose were those I thought might appeal to those listening. I came to know, that in the various clubs I was playing in, I had my own little fan clubs, people who hoped I might be playing when they stopped in to hear the music. And so I came to play for them more and more, knowing I couldn't play jazz as I wanted, but they were telling me that I must be doing something right – and as long as the people liked it, I always got invited to come back, by whomever the musicians were. So I guess I was doing something right with them also. But the audience is always important. They will tell you if you are a good player. They are the judges – not you!

One of the groups I played with at Marmacs and other clubs was tenorman Rex Davis. He was adequate and could really "honk". He was a good showman, and popular wherever he played. I guess I played with him for 3-4 years. I always remember him inviting me to get up and play, saying, "Bring home the bread, Fred"! Those were part of my "learning how to play jazz" years – so I jump ahead to 1986

I was in a music shop buying a "fake book", the books of

music containing only the lead sheets of music, containing two handed melody and bass lines, and the lyrics. I can't read music, but that was the only way to learn the lyrics to various songs. I met Rex whom I hadn't seen for a long time. He offered me a job playing in a new club. He told me to name my own price, he didn't care, just name my price! What a surprise for this wannabe musician! He knew, that after all my years of playing non jazz with him, I had finally became a good jazz player! What a great thrill in that offer. I knew professional guys playing for 30 dollars a nite – and he's offering me whatever I want!!

When I finally learned to play jazz, I visited all the clubs and groups I had played with. I wanted them to know I could finally play jazz. No one made the comment, "you finally made it"! – but I knew by the grins, big smiles, high fives, and playing full sets instead of 2-3 numbers, that they knew I was a jazz player, and all were tickled and happy with everything we played – Satin Doll, "A" Train, and an up tempo "Lil Darlin", and many more, Bossa Novas. Just as they never commented on my failings – they never commented on my success. Their actions spoke for themselves. I told each that it was their encouragement, and never putting me down, and all else they had done for me, was the reason of my success in playing jazz!!

During the mid 70's the music scene began to change in my area. What once had been nice restazurants and cocktail lounges, now became beer bars frequented and owned by Latinos. A few had Latin bands. Learning Latin music as played by the big bands in the 30's and 40's by Xavier Cugat, Enrique Madriguera, Luis Arcaraz, and many other American swing bands, and all the top vocalists, as Crosby, Cole, Eberly and others, opened me up to this music. Knowing much of this I went into these Latin clubs to listen to a music I liked very much. Most times I was greeted with suspicion, as many of the Latin people were illegal immigrants, and were scared I might be from the office of Immigration and was there to bust illegals. It took awhile before they understood I was there only to hear the music on their juke boxes.

Eventually I made friends with many, and did get to play in a few Latin bands. They were surprised at all the Latin music I knew, and liked my playing.

I would like to relate a few important incidents of my not only getting to know Latin music, but the musicians and people I met in that community of strangers, who eventually became my good friends.

Back in the 50's I listened to a DJ in Boston who handled the radio chores from 6 P.M. til sundown. He played a closing theme for 6 months until the change from daylight saving time to his final program when the station went off the air in October's Standard Time.

He said he had received thousands of letters, asking who the band was that played the closing theme, as it was different and a bit ahead of its time, with a wonderful different approach to playing the old chestnut, "Johnson Rag". He said the band was from Mexico – Luis Arcaraz. I had never heard of him and I doubt any others did either. I went out and found 3 records of Luis Arcaraz, learned about him then, and much later when I moved to the Los Angeles area where I found more of his music. Though most people liked Pres. Prado, my favorite Latin band has always been Luis Arcaraz. His band arrangements of Latin music were more akin to American big band arrangements, with excellent soloists. Many songs were American standards played with a Latin influence. To this day I continue to play his recordings.

So listening to Arcaraz, and having bought bongo and conga drums, claves, and other rhythmic Latin instruments, and practicing playing them, I was ready to play the music.

One club I played in jam sessions on Sunday was "El Chapparal". Friday and Saturday they featured 6 piece Latin group – I think a few were illegals as they spoke almost no "English", and I spoke no Spanish. But I got to know and play with them – the music was our common language.

I also played with 2 other groups in Latin clubs and it was a very rewarding experience. In the first group of older musicians, one tenor sax man was an excellent musician, but not proficient in jazz. He asked me if I wanted to go out with him to visit clubs in L.A. All this translated to me by his buddies who spoke a little more English. So we went out to all the clubs where he played in L.A., an area I wouldn't ever be in at night alone! But he knew many people – introduced me to all, seeming to be very proud to have me as his friend. He and all I met made me feel special! We didn't play music wherever we went, I think he was trying to show me how popular he was in all these clubs we visited, and at the same time introducing this "Gringo" who knew and played so much Latin music. I not only met musicians and his fans, but also met all the club owners. I really felt special! We spent the whole night in these clubs, conversing in less than a dozen words or less, of each others language and many hand signals and motions. We became excellent friends. He was a well schooled musician, Cirio Baray, and played piano, violin, all the woodwinds, and very excellently!

The biggest thrill for me was their inviting me to some sort of Latin Fiesta in Oxnard, California, a drive of around 100 miles. We got there early in the A.M. I (slept?) on a couch at a Latino family's home, they fed us breakfast, and were great hosts. We went to a great big place, it reminded me of an old Movie Theater, we sat in the balcony which surrounded the inside of the building, as did other bands. We each took turns playing for about an hour. I never did count the number of bands that played. I was the only "Gringo" there!

Then it came time for Cirio's band, and they played their set. I was called to do two solo's, one a song they taught me "Sabor a me" and "Flora Negra", I had heard in the 30's and 40's. I got a great ovation from the audience. More than my playing, what thrilled and overwhelmed me was the fact, here is this lone "Gringo" playing for an audience of a couple of thousand Latino people, in the biggest venue in my life, and all these strangers liked my music, and treated me as one of them. It has to be one of the top musical experiences of my life!

I would like to relate a few incidents of my attempting to chase my dream of being a jazz player, to advise those who have aspirations seeming out of sight, yet with a sincere desire and effort, can realize that very dream. It can be a long, and frustrating road.

While sitting in at Marmacs Dinnerhouse with Buddy Banks, he couldn't make it one weekend as he was sick. Another group filled in. The leader was well known, a drummer I only knew as "Rabon". He co-authored a very popular tune called "Cement'Mixer, Putti Putti". I did a couple of tunes with him, as by that time I was a regular "sit in" customer. He told me he was opening at a club in Valley View, and would I come down to help out on opening nite? I went to the club, and waited through 2 sets, wondering if he forgot me. After the second set he came up to me saying, "you're going to do the next set with this guy,"introducing me to a piano player who's name I've long forgotten. (Excuse the lack of memory in my old age.) He told me the piano man had just returned from Europe with the Lionel Hampton Band. I thought ' – oh, baby, I'm going to play with Hamp's piano man'? I wasn't ready to do a jazz set – I couldn't play jazz – I was really scared, figuring I'm really going to blow this gig!

I only remember the first song, "Stella by Starlight" – everything else is a blur in my memory – I was so uptight and nervous, I just don't remember what we played on the whole set! When we finished, I went back to the bar, and bought him a drink. He said to me, "I've heard just about every harmonica player there is. You're the best I've ever heard". I was amazed and very surprised! All I could do was tell him the truth, and said, "Man I was just trying to stay with you"! In truth, the reason I can't remember what we played, is because I played way over my head, above my ability, but somehow, just listening to the chords he was laying down, must have instinctively played all the right notes in soloing jazz choruses! I can't explain it – but there were occasions when I did play over my head, but could never remember what in heck I played – but I had played very well. And with a compliment like that, it only encourages one to keep trying until you know you got it right – and you remember what you did. I learned one thing that night – always play with musicians better than I. This enabled me to stretch, to reach out to play on the plateau where they were, resulting in more learning and becoming a better player.

A couple of years later I was playing with Bill March at "Sileo's", an Italian dinnerhouse in Long Beach, CA. After a couple of hours playing, Bill took a break. I waited for Bill to return to the piano bar and when he finally did he told me he had been talking to a customer at a dinner table, and the customer remarked on how much he enjoyed our music. I said, "Why not, you're an excellent musician". Bill said, "He wasn't talking about me, he was complimenting you, he said your playing is the best he's heard". I told Bill that was a nice compliment. Then Bill said, "You know who it was? – Charlie Ventura!" Charlie Ventura!! Wow! Gene Krupa's long time great tenor sax man! I had seen him at "Birdland", in New York City when he was the featured guest for the week. I would like to have met him, but he had left the club, having finished his dinner. Man what a nice thing to hear – and this coming at a time when I still didn't know how to play jazz! Do you wonder why I continued to play? Who wouldn't, with compliments like that! Simply overwhelming!

Somewhere around 1977 I played with the Smiley Wilson group in Long Beach at "Hogan's East". Smiley had been on the "Buck Owens *Hee Haw* television show" for some years. Buck played strictly country western music. Smiley played fiddle, a mini-guitar, and trombone, all very well. Smiley told me, when he heard Stan Kenton, that was the end of Buck Owens! In his jazz group, Smiley always ended a set with a "hoe down" number and holler wah-hee!! "That's hee-haw backward"!

In playing with Smiley, a fellow came up to me and said I was better than the #1 harmonica player in the world! Now that's a compliment! I am glad I only took remarks like that as merely a nice bit of praise. Thank God, I never got an ego. How could I really take something like that to heart when I knew I couldn't play jazz? The nice things only told me I was doing something right, and were statements enough to keep me playing, and though these compliments were nice to hear, my mind told me one thing – 'gee I wish I could really play'! But again – no time for a 'big head', just keep trying. Maybe some day all those nice things said to me will be justified when I learn to play jazz right. I desperately wanted to "play like other horn players". I had heard so many other musicians tell me, "Fred, I don't know what in heck you're doing but you are always around the melody". And that was so true – there was just no continuity to any of my attempts at soloing, not having that knack of understanding how to improvise. I usually got lost in my soloing, and only in listening to the other musicians, did I know when to end my solo! I was very discouraged with myself, and if it hadn't been for the many compliments received, I would have quit in the very beginning. Thanks to all the caring feeling musicians who kept encouraging me - I stayed with it. Maybe someday I thought.

I would like to relate some of the frustrations associated with attempting to play music in my beginning days of going out to clubs in the hopes I would be allowed to play.

In addition to playing clubs, I have attended my Air Force Reunions all over the U.S. So since 1969 we have always had either a big band or small jazz groups at our banquets, and other activities, playing our kind of music from the 40's – the Swing Era. I have played with nearly all these groups – my "on the road" days!

One reunion in 1976, at Tarpon Springs, Florida, I met my Bomber pilot for the first time since he had been shot down in November '43, over Greece – which is another great story. We were on a boat cruise of Tampa Bay, and a Dixieland Band were entertaining us. I remarked to my pilot how I'd like to play with them. As officers and enlisted men weren't allowed to fraternize in the service, he had never heard me play. He left the table, and returned about 10 minutes later saying, "I just gave the band leader 10 bucks to hear you play". So I went to talk to the leader and told him I played harmonica. Immediately I got all the excuses why I couldn't play – except the real reason – harmonica was a no-no in a jazz band! I told him he sounded like a "Bostonian", which he admitted to. I asked where in the Boston area, and he said, "Chelsea". I said, "that's where I'm from, what's your name?" "Zaitz", he replied. "Zaitz! I know your brother, he plays drums at the VFW – in fact your folks own the bakery where my Mom and I bought our baked goods – in fact your family catered my sisters wedding"! All this was true! He replied, "What would you like to play"! So neighborly ties was the only reason he let me play, and it surprised me and the group to the extent, I played a whole set and they loved it! My first lesson in the harmonica being disliked by jazz players! I would experience the same reluctance later with Dick Carey and others, until I learned never to tell them what instrument I played, but instead asking them if I could play a well known jazz song, and when they said, sure – it was too late when I would pull out my harmonica and once they heard me, that was my OK to play anytime!

In 1977 the Clef Club had it's annual jazz festival on Catalina Island. We took a boat to the Island, a running jam session going on all the way from Long Beach over to Catalina, even the musicians parading to Avalon Ballroom, a la New Orleans style. It was a great fun time. At the ballroom bands were featured every half hour for the time we were there. I was scheduled to play with a group, but there were so many groups there, time ran out before all the groups could play, so my first chance at playing a jazz festival was postponed for a year.

So in 1978 I played my first jazz festival at the Monterey Park Country Club. It was a thrill to see my name on the playbill, along side all the well known jazz musicians. I took my turn and played with a piano, bass and drums, with a fine alto sax backing me up, and also swapping solos, doing a nice set which pleased the listeners. To say it was a big thrill is an understatement. And even though I still couldn't manage a coherent solo, everything worked out fine. At that time it was the high point of my life, and made for easier access to playing in other clubs as the musicians at the festival liked my playing, though at that time I was a pretty good player, but not a jazz player yet.

One note – As I state I played with many guys in the various clubs for many years – these aren't 7 days a week, but rather years of weekend playing, mainly 3 nights, sometimes a bit more, but my main job was as a mechanic, enabling me to afford the weekend playing.

One thing I never did was take money for playing, even though I played gigs where we got a paying job. One such time was when a trombonist friend, Tom Neher, had a big band and also a small group. He had a gig at the Elks Club in Santa Ana, to play a Christmas Party. I was part of the group. We played one set, and were into the second set when an alarm came to evacuate the club, as someone said a bomb was discovered. I looked at the beautiful Christmas decorations throughout the hall as we exited the club. We waited in a club across the street while the police and firemen did their jobs. They never did find a bomb, and by that time it was 2 AM, so we never played again that night. We were paid 50 bucks a man anyway. I gave my share to the other guys, as my thank you for all they had done for me. And as I had a good steady job I didn't need the money, they did. Most only worked at music for 30 bucks a night on average, some had part time, or no other jobs, so I did not mind contributing my end to those who had helped me with my music goal.

Another time to help these musicians came about from my frequenting a nice dinner house in the area of Lake Isabella in the southern Sierra's. I visited the area on many weeks, or weekends, as it was my future home where I intended to retire to in the mountains. The owner of the dinner house loved big bands and jazz, so I told him I could get some guys to come up for a night. He said he could only afford 250 dollars. So I got Tom

Neher to bring a few guys up to the lake, and we played a nice gig, ate at the dinner house, had a cottage to sleep in, and had a real good session, pleasing the owner. I played for nothing. The guys made a few bucks and also enjoyed the mountain area, even though it was 150 miles from L.A. On the way home we held an impromptu jam session in a country/western bar, and the patrons loved it!

Sometime in the early 80's Tom Neher told me he wanted me to go to a club in Carson, CA., 'The Chatroom'. He told me there was a harmonica player there and he wanted me to "blow him out of the room". I said I couldn't do that, but it was another opportunity to play at a new club, so I went there.

A harmonica player did a whole set, and I said to myself, "this guy is great! And I'm supposed to blow him out of the room? He was intimidating!" So much so that my lack of confidence kicked in and I didn't play at all. (Tom later told me, that wasn't the harmonica player he was talking about!) I never again let anyone intimidate me!

(He was a well known jazz harmonica player, who had won 1st prize on the Gong Show twice – he was great! Named Thompson.)

All week long the thought of being intimidated nagged at me for being such a mental coward. So I was determined to go back and play whether he was there or not. When I went there the following week, I saw him sitting in a car outside the club, and I decided to let him know how much I felt about being intimidated the previous week, and that I didn't care how good he was, I was going to play!

I played a full set as he had done, and I played one of my better performances. I felt vindicated and confident. He didn't play – and I often wondered if he was being nice to me by not playing, and just letting me do my own thing. I never met him again – but he is great!

Once I called Arnie Berquist whom I first played with in 1970. He said he was working in a 'pizza parlor' in Hollywood, so I had Tom, Carl Ogden trumpet man, go with me to see Arnie. A nephew of old time band leader Tiny Hill, was playing drums, and another fellow playing clarinet. So we had a nice jam session. In looking around the place was full of Latino's. So I suggested to Arnie, we play some Latin tunes. We played all the old 40's tunes, 'Yours', 'Besame Mucho', 'Green Eyes', and many others. The people started coming up putting tips on the piano, there was no tip jar. By the time we left, the piano was flooded with dollar bills – at least 100 bucks. Arnie wanted to give it to us, but we said no. I was pleased to do something for Arnie to repay him in one small way for all his early encouragement of me – and besides, I had a million dollars worth of fun just playing, and being with a good friend again to help him!

I only played in Hollywood three times, with Arnie Berquist, and once at the Dresden Room, where I sat in with a piano, bass duo, whose names I didn't know, but did OK, furthering my learning experience.

The other interesting time was during the day, when I saw a sign in front of an Italian Restaurant advertising a special on lasagna! So I parked, went in to order and have a drink. There was a young guy playing piano. He sounded very good, so I asked if I could play with him while I waited for my meal. In those early days I always had a harmonica in my car – just in case! So I brought it in and we did a whole bunch of tunes. Upon his asking, I gave him my name, and he told me who he was. He was the fellow who played "Peter" on the old *"Mickey Mouse Club"* on TV, with Annette Funicello. He was a very talented pianist and I enjoyed playing with him.

My only near brush with a chance to record came when I played at Paramount, CA., the "Ports-O-Call" dinner house music lounge. I played back-up for many singers, and they all liked it. One night in playing, a young woman came in who's name is long forgotten now, but she was a pretty successful songwriter in the 70's. She wanted the band to go to Hollywood to do some recording and wanted me to play backup. So at 1 AM we went to the studio. I waited for 4 ½ hours as they argued about where they were going to place all the microphones. After waiting all those hours, I looked at the time – 6:30 AM, told them I had to be to work at 7, and left the studio, never went back and never heard from anyone, regarding the recording. That was probably my only chance of recording – which at times I regret.

In my playing music from 1970 to the 90's, I would bring a tape recorder with me, so I could listen to the tapes critically, hopefully to find out what I was doing wrong, for there were mistakes enough to ruin what could have been good playing.

Most times the tape recorder would sit there and I would forget to turn it on. In all the years of playing in the dozens of clubs, I taped myself about 12 times and in only 7 venues. So all I have are seven 90 minute tapes of my music, and only 3 of music after I learned to solo jazz choruses.

Many times I've been asked by various people, if I record as they like my music. I tell them the truth – it's my favorite hobby.

On a trip to our old stomping grounds with my WWII buddies on a trip overseas, we stayed at the Palace Hotel in Sorrento, Italy. They had a great big lounge and dance floor, with a good pianist. I asked him if I could play with him. Though his English and my Italian was limited, we both knew the music. I played with him for 1 ½ hours playing French, Italian, Latin, Bossa Nova and yes, jazz! Many foreign people from other countries, staying at the hotel, asked me if I recorded, and pleasantly surprised at their interest, I had to tell them it was only a hobby, my realizing, hey, I missed the big bubble.

I've played at my Air Force reunions all over the country and am asked by other musicians from big bands and small groups, and I have to give them the same answer, as wherever I go, people like my playing and assume I am a recording artist. Very complimentary!

CHAPTER 5
How I Learned to Play Jazz

I must give much credit to Bill March, with whom I played for a half dozen years. Bill would let me join in on any song he played, as he had an extra mike hooked up, and so I began playing with him every weekend.

Bill gave me a double set of video tapes of Duke Ellington, containing many accolades about Duke from other musicians, much music of his band, and much comment from Duke concerning music and musicians.

Duke made the comment that every musician is limited. He gave one good example of a famous musician who was a favorite of mine, and his limitations. Duke went on to say, "I can take the first chair of any symphony orchestra, and that man will be limited"!

I said to myself, "H'mmm – I can't play songs with difficult key changes – so I'm limited. Then I mused, well if I know 1000 songs and can only play 900, that's not too bad, I'll just play what I can handle". That was my first lesson.

I also have a nice collection of jazz artists who were the

innovators of jazz music, Ellington, Armstrong, Goodman and about 30 other icons. In reading a biography contained in every container of 3 LP's, of Coleman Hawkins, the great tenor sax player, a fan asked him how he could play so many choruses without repeating himself. Hawkins replied, pointing to his thumb and fingers one by one, "I play the melody, the harmony to that, and the harmony to that, and the harmony to that," touching each finger as he spoke, saying, "and I just keep going".

It hit me right between the eyes, *"that's how you do it"!!* It had been there and I didn't see it! If I hadn't been too ashamed to ask, I probably could have played jazz years ago!

I decided I would try to play improvised choruses the next time I went to play with Bill March the following weekend. This time I did remember to turn on my tape recorder. Everything turned out well, the first time I learned to play jazz correctly! This is my favorite tape! It is my "collectors item" – my coming out party playing jazz! From that night on, I have never been afraid to play with anyone! I may not be as proficient as some horn player – but I'll be right there! It had been a long time coming, much frustration, disappointing times, but I did it – I was a success in my first love – music! I was 63 years old – I felt 20! The many comments by the audience also told me I had finally reached that plateau where other jazz horn players enjoyed the freedom to improvise, "ad lib" solos. What a nice feeling and period of relaxation in playing. I had to show other musicians I had played with early on, that I had made it. I visited them at their clubs and played real jazz, and could tell from their exuberant comments and happy attitude toward me, that they also knew I had finally made it in jazz.

I played many more clubs in the Long Beach area, too many to count, for about 2 years and during that time the Artie Shaw band came to California. I knew Dick Johnson the leader as he was a good friend of my brother, who was with the public relations side of the band.

While they were here, I sponsored a jam session at "The

Speakeasy" where I had been playing for a few years with Bill March. I catered the meal, 5 guys from the Shaw band came to jam and I had a ball playing with them, especially Lou Columbo, fine lead trumpet, who was the "Billy Butterfield" of the trumpet section, as Lou played all the early solo spots that Billy had played on Shaw's early hits. Shaw wasn't at the jam session, but I did get to meet him a few times. I wasn't too impressed with him as a person, especially his harboring the same jealousy and dislike for Benny Goodman for the last 30 years!

At my peak playing music, I retired from my regular job and moved to Lake Isabella in the southern Sierra Mountains, a series of small towns surrounded the Lake. In the beginning of 1986, there were a lot of places to play some good jazz, and I played just about every joint and club in the area, but jazz is not an art form the locals like. The musical style deteriorated to karaoke singing, country western and rock, so playing with these people unschooled in jazz was disappointing, so that I don't play outside anymore, I have to satisfy myself by playing along with LP's or CD's at home, alone.

One brief spell of good music occurred when a good guitarist came to the Lake area, hoping to find a gig. I sat in with him one night and we became good friends. In the intial days of playing with him, he told me "I don't like ballads, I don't like swing, Bossa Nova, Latin music"! When he finished telling me all his "don't likes", there was only one thing left – be-bop! And that's what he played. Be-bop is pretty difficult music, especially on a harmonica, so I could only do what I had been doing for years – stretching my musical muscles to reach his plateau. After much struggle I did play this difficult style, but am not partial to this style of playing. But it didn't last only a few months, as Joe Olinghouse, the be-bop guitarist left the area for greener pastures. Bill Hess, flugel horn and trombone, was part of our little trio, but he too left to move to Florida.

Before I close out this treatise of my musical experience, I would like to write of the only times I was put down by musicians. Both incidents resulted in being humorous of sorts.

Way back when – living in Massachusetts, I visited my brother Don on Cape Cod. We went to a club to hear Bobby Hackett and Dave McKenna, trumpet and piano jazz greats. After the club session Dave and another pianist, and a bass player and I went back to my brother's house. Dave McKenna had already consumed over a fifth of vodka at the club. So he wasn't in the best shape.

My brother suggested he and I play a few tunes in the den. So we started playing a pretty ballad. Before we were half way through the song, Dave started pounding the piano keys with his elbows, ruining the playing. I said, "Famous piano player or not, I don't need this crap"! And I walked out of the room. I was put out but not angry, as I realized Dave was drunk, and that was the way he acted at that time. The bass player and the other pianist were very angry – especially the bass player. He told a story of a time when he was put down. To be brief – he had been a band member of a small group, and like me was a self taught musician. His regular job was as a plumber. At the end of the night the group leader went to the club owner to collect the pay for the group. The owner paid all except the bass player, saying, "He stinks and I won't pay him". Well, they went round and round for quite a while, always with the same result – everyone gets paid except the bass player, with much cussing going on in this crazy conversation. Finally the bass player spoke up, "I'm asking you in a nice way – I worked all night, and I can't help it if you think I played bad, I worked just as the others, and I should get paid, so I'm asking one more time – are you going to pay me?" The club owner, using every curse word in the book, ended by saying, "If you don't get your --- out of here, I'll throw your --- --- --- out the ---- door!" So the bass player said OK and left.

The next morning the club owner went down to open the club, and all he saw was a pile of burnt embers – no nite club. As he stood there in shock and amazement at the ruins of his nite club – the bass player walked up to him and said, "Now do I get paid?" ------ As well as being a plumber and wannabe bass player, he also had ties to the Mafia!!

After that little story, the bass player and the other piano player left my brothers house, I followed about ½ hour later. When I got outside the bass and piano man were waiting, and stated they were waiting for Dave McKenna to come out of my brother's house. They were still intensely angry over his treatment of me, and told me in no uncertain terms, "We are going to break his f---- fingers so he'll never play piano again"!! Evidently both were fringe Mafia figures, and kept ranting about Dave, and what they were going to do to him. I pleaded with them not to bother, I wasn't angry, Dave was drunk, he was really an OK guy, everything I could think of to prevent harm to Dick. It took a good hour to calm them down. I breathed a great big sigh of relief when we shook hands, they agreeing not to harm Dave, and I left hoping they would keep their word.

Evidently they did, for that was 40-50 years ago, and Dave has gone on to be one of the best jazz pianists, playing with various jazz groups all over the country at countless jazz festivals and venues.

I never told anyone – I wonder what Dave would say if he knew his future was saved by a lowly harmonica player he had snubbed!

The other incident occurred when my son and I went to a club to hear the jazz music in Revere, Mass. Another bass player, whom I had played with in East Boston, recognized me and told the drummer band leader of my being there, and I assume, telling him of my jazz playing ability. What made the situation so funny, is that the drummer left his microphone "on", and didn't realize it, so everything heard was with many "F" words being heard when he was being convinced of my ability, such as, "we're playing "F" jazz, who in "F" needs a "F" harmonica player. On and on, over and over, until he let this "F" harmonica player "F" play. Everybody in this big club could hear him, and they were in a hilarious mood. As it was the final number and closing time, I only played one song, "Meditation", the pretty Bossa Nova. The crowd loved it! I went back to the bar to join my son. The drummer came up to me, apologizing for being, a bad drummer, "I'm a show drummer, I'm not a good jazz drummer, I don't know Bossa Nova, excuse me if I missed the boat," and on and and on, sounding more ridiculous the longer he made excuses. I have to say it was one of the funniest "F" times in playing "F" jazz!!

Joe Olinghouse had me playing "Be-Bop", 1995

CHAPTER 6
Coda

I had to look up the word 'coda' in the dictionary to make sure of its meaning!

Of prime importance to me is the eternal "Thank you" I must say to all the fine musicians I played with, the encouragement, the countless invitations to play, the always positive comments, and the great friendships that developed between us. They are a great part of my success in learning to play a "horn"!

I would firmly think my most important thank you must go to God. HE gave me the talent for music. He gave me the talent as a mechanic, also proven by my success in that field.

He gave me the talent to write. I have written four books, two on my WWII experiences, one on corruption, and this book. Am I a great writer? No, but I'm not a great musician either. But just as people like *WHAT* I play, they also like *WHAT* I write. And just as in the music, if the people like what you have accomplished that in of itself is success.

Did I ever make money from my accomplishments? Only in the mechanical field, and that in my weeks pay.

So how do you measure success?

My Dad was also disappointed in me because I didn't play sports. I was too small. When I entered High School, I weighed 90 pounds, and was less than 5 feet – the average guy on the team was over 200 pounds.

I did play baseball and football in the service, because I grew. I'm a late bloomer. I did do things my Dad never did. I played football when I was 50 – I got roughed up pretty bad, but I DID IT! – even scored a touchdown, even though my team lost!

I played softball until I was 70 – my batting average was well over 500 – we lost the final game and the championship, and I couldn't buy a hit! But I DID IT!

Success is also in the *DOING*. It is just as any guy playing baseball, and always dreaming of hitting a home run. Finally after many years he finally does, even though his team loses. But he finally realizes he reached his dream, his goal. He hit a home run! So the team lost – so what – He succeeded! Reaching the seemingly impossible dream – is the ultimate Success!

Because I never got to play what I wanted in my first 4 years of life, I developed a message that I would impress on everyone.

"Do what *you* want to do, as long as you don't hurt yourself or anyone else, do what you love best."

I always used a work ethic that I believe in. I worked as though I owned the business. I did a job as quick as I could, I did it once, I did it right! And so, doing it right is most important, and the ethic I wanted in my music.

So how do you measure success?

Some years ago I cut out a message written by the old leader of India, Mahatma Gandhi, and though I wasn't into philosophical messages at the time, it definitely was at the time I decided to try playing music in the clubs. Somehow the message resonated with me. The message is as follows –

MEASURE OF A MAN

*It is not the critic who counts, nor the man who points
out how the strong man stumbles, or where the doer
of deeds could have done better, the credit belongs
to the man who is actually in the arena; who's face
is marred by dust and sweat; who strives valiantly;
who errs and may fail again, because there is no effort
without error or shortcoming, but does actually strive to do the
deeds; who does know the great enthusiasm, the great
devotion; who spends himself in a worthy cause; who
at the best, knows in the end the triumph of high achievement,
and who at the worst, if he fails, at least fails while
daring greatly, so his place shall never be with those cold
and timid souls who know neither victory nor defeat.*
—*Mahatma Gandhi*

So how do you measure success? I measure it in the finality of reaching your original goal. I did that. I never chased the star of fame. I did what I set out to do, and I did it. Thanks to all the God-given talent, I've done much I never expected to do, with much thanks to others in all aspects of my life.

Are you a "wannabe"? GO DO IT!!

At a private party

For Free CD:

Frederick Lawrence
P.O. Box 376
Wofford Heights, CA 93285